The Movement Game

Written by
Andrea Lambertson
Illustrated by Linda M. Gangian

Print information available on the last page

Rev. date: 07/09/2019

To order additional copies of this book, contact:
Xlibris
1-888-795-4274
www.Xlibris.com
Orders@Xlibris.com

This book is dedicated
to all the children of the
Private and Public Schools of America.

May you all move through
a healthy, successful and happy life.

Susie and Bobby went to school
First day for them and so many rules
All subjects were fun: English, Spelling, Math, History,
Science, Music, Art and Gym.
Yes, all were new to them and they could not wait
to begin.

Two days a week the specialists arrive
Wow, were they in for a fun surprise!
The bell rang and it was time for art.
They drew pictures, painted, they felt creative and smart.
Music began and they sang and sang,
Played the flute and drum
Boy, was that fun!

Next class PE, Physical Education, Gym, all words
mean the same:
Movement is the name of the game.
We can move our bodies in so many different ways,
Is it not truly fun to play?

When we are sick we usually stay in bed
To rest our bodies and our heads
We can not move then
It is hard for our bodies even to bend.
But with rest and nutritious foods
We can soon get up and continue to move again.

Joe Namath of Football fame,

Billy Jean King, Tennis is her game.

Ballet dancers and Baseball stars,

All love to move from the ground to the sky.

We can move almost anyway, except it is rather hard,

Actually impossible to *fly*.

Birds move by flapping their wings

Deer leap over fences and things

Rabbits jump

Snakes crawl

Fish swim

We as human beings, children and adults, can do all these things.

Yes, movement is a super groovy thing
If we stay physically fit
We can play the Movement Game throughout the
summer, fall, winter, and spring.

Our bodies are short, tall
Sometimes big, sometimes small.
No matter what our size
We must try the Movement Game and be happily
surprised!

So whether you are 2, 4, 6, 8, or 10
45, 55, 65- Yes, even then
Movement should never, never and.

The End

Printed in the United States
By Bookmasters